To

From

---

10 Types of
COURTSHIP

10 Types of
COURTSHIP

FEMI OYEWOPO

ACHIEVERS WORLD

10 Types of Courtship
Copyright © 2019 by Femi Oyewopo.
All rights reserved.

Requests for information should be addressed to:
femioyewopo@gmail.com

This book, or parts thereof, may not be reproduced, stored in a retrieval system, or transmitted in any form or by any means, electronic, mechanical, photocopying,
recording or otherwise, without the written permission of the publisher.

ISBN 978-0-6482834-3-0 (paperback)
ISBN 978-0-6482834-9-2 (ebook)

Printed in Australia

Acknowledgments:

Every attempt has been made to credit the sources of copyrighted material used in this book. If any such acknowledgment has been inadvertently omitted or miscredited, receipt of such information would be appreciated

Unless otherwise indicated, all Scripture quotations are taken from the Holy Bible New King James Version, © 1979, 1980, 1982, 1984 by Thomas Nelson, Inc. Used by permission. All rights reserved.
Scripture quotations marked (CEB) are taken from the *Common English Bible.* Copyright © 2011 by Common English Bible.
Scripture quotations marked (CEV) are taken from *Holy Bible: Contemporary English Version.* Copyright © 1995 American Bible Society.
Scripture quotations marked (ESV) are taken from the *Holy Bible, English Standard Version*, copyright © 2001 by Crossway Bibles, a division of Good News Publishers. Used by permission. All rights reserved.
Scripture quotations marked (GNT) are taken from the *Holy Bible, Good News Translation.* Copyright © 1992 by American Bible Society.
Scripture quotations marked (ISV) are taken from the *Holy Bible, International Standard Version.* Copyright © 1995–2014 by ISV Foundation. All rights reserved internationally. Used by permission of Davidson Press, LLC. Scripture quotations marked (KJV) are taken from the *King James Version of the Bible.*
Scripture quotations marked (MSG) are taken from *The Message.* Copyright © 1993, 1994, 1995, 1996, 2000, 2001, 2002 by Eugene H. Peterson.
Scripture quotations marked (NAS) are taken from the *New American Standard Bible*, copyright © 1960, 1962, 1963, 1968, 1971, 1972, 1973, 1975, 1977, 1995 by the Lockman Foundation. Used by permission.
Scripture quotations marked (NCV) are taken from *The Holy*

Bible, New Century Version. Copyright © 2005 by Thomas Nelson, Inc.

Scripture quotations marked (NIrV) are taken from *New International Reader's Version*. Copyright © 1995, 1996, 1998, 2014 by Biblica, Inc.® Used by permission. All rights reserved worldwide.

Scripture quotations marked (NIV) are taken from *The Holy Bible, New International Version*. Copyright © 1973, 1978, 1984, 2011 by Biblica, Inc.® Used by permission of Zondervan. All rights reserved worldwide. www.Zondervan.com.

Scripture quotations marked (NKJV) are taken from *The Holy Bible, New King James Version*. Copyright © 1982 by Thomas Nelson, Inc.

Scripture quotations marked (NLT) are from the *Holy Bible, New Living Translation*. Copyright © 1996, 2004, 2007 by Tyndale House Foundation. Used by permission of Tyndale House Publishers Inc., Carol Stream, Illinois 60188. All rights reserved.

Scripture quotations marked (NRSV) are taken from the *New Revised Standard Version Bible*. Copyright © 1989 by the Division of Christian Education of the National Council of the Churches of Christ in the United States of America. Used by permission. All rights reserved.

Scripture quotations marked (RSV) are taken from the *Revised Standard Version of the Bible*. Copyright © 1946, 1952, 1971 by Division of Christian Education of the National Council of Churches of Christ in the United States of America. Used by permission.

Scripture quotations marked (TLB) are taken from *The Living Bible*. Copyright © 1971 by Tyndale House Publishers, Wheaton, Illinois 60188. All rights reserved.

Words and phrases in Scripture quotations that are in **bold** or *italics* are the emphasis of the author.

DOWNLOAD THE TOOLBOX FREE

Just to say thanks for buying my book, I would like to give you the Ultimate Self Discovery Toolbox version 100% FREE!

TO DOWNLOAD GO TO:
http://femioyewopo.com/21ipop_toolbox

Great Quotes about Courtship & Marriage

'My boyfriend used to ask his mother, "How can I find the right woman for me?" She would answer, "Don't worry about finding the right woman – concentrate on becoming the right man."'
- (Unknown)

'Woman was taken out of man; not out of his head to top him, nor out of his feet to be trampled underfoot; but out of his side to be equal to him, under his arm to be protected, and near his heart to be loved.' **- (Unknown)**

'Flatter me and I may not believe you. Criticise me and I may not like you. Encourage me and I will not forget you. Love me and I may love you.' **- (Unknown)**

If you have to lower your moral standard to find love, then it is not love that you are finding. **- Jason Evert**

I believe the Bible to teach that all sexual activity outside of marriage is sin, and all romantically oriented physical activity is sexual activity. In my view, this includes premarital kissing.
- Scott Croft

"Falling in love in a Christian way is to say, 'I am excited about your future and I want to be part of getting you there. I'm signing up for the journey with you. Would you sign up for the journey to my true self with me? It's going to be hard but I want to get there." **- Tim Keller**

DEDICATION

This book is dedicated to my one and only
beautiful, loving, caring,
prayerful and highly supportive wife,

Oludotun Adesola Omolewa.

You are my number one cheerleader.

This book would not have been possible

without your constant support and encouragement.
Thank you for being my accountability buddy.

I love you *and* I will always love you.

CONTENTS

Acknowledgments | 7

Dedication | 13

Introduction | 19

Chapter 1
DATING -- 21

Chapter 2
ENGAGEMENT -------------------------------------- 7

Chapter 3
COURTSHIP -- 43

Chapter 4
TRIANGLE OF
SUCCESSFUL RELATIONSHIPS ----------------- 57

PART B
Types of Courtship

Chapter 5
COURTSHIP 1:
WRONG COURTSHIP ------------------------------ 67

Chapter 6
COURTSHIP 2:
PURPOSELESS COURTSHIP ---------------------- 73

Chapter 7
COURTSHIP 3:
CARRY OVER COURTSHIP ---------------------- 79

Chapter 8
COURTSHIP 4:
NICODEMUS COURTSHIP ---------------------- 85

Chapter 9
COURTSHIP 5:
CLOSED COURTSHIP ------------------------------ 91

Chapter 10
COURTSHIP 6:
CAPTIVE COURTSHIP ---------------------------- 97

Chapter 11
COURTSHIP 7:
UNCLEAN COURTSHIP -------------------------- 103

Chapter 12
COURTSHIP 8:
DRY COURTSHIP ---------------------------------- 111

Chapter 13
COURTSHIP 9:
ARRANGED COURTSHIP ---------------------- 117

Chapter 14
COURTSHIP 10:
BALANCED COURTSHIP ------------------------ 125

Chapter 15
HOW TO HAVE
A BALANCED COURTSHIP ---------------------- 129

Chapter 16
HOW TO BE SAVED ------------------------------ 133

INTRODUCTION

Dr. James Dobson, the president of *Focus on the Family* once said that there are three major decisions you will ever make in your lifetime:

1. Whom you will serve—God, the Devil or self.

   "No man can serve two masters..." **(Matthew 6:24).**

2. What career you will pursue.

3. To whom you will marry and spend the rest of your life.

"It is not good for a man to be alone..." **(Genesis 2:18).**

> ...there are three major decisions you will ever make in your lifetime:

I strongly believe that these three decisions will heavily impact your destiny, not only in this life but also in eternity. Decision Determines Destiny.

In this book, *The Ten Types of Courtship*, we will be

INTRODUCTION

focusing on the process of making the third choice: deciding who to spend the rest of your life with. Marriage is not an end in itself but a means to an end. God made it clear what His original intention was and why He instituted marriage:

"It is not good that the man should be alone; I will make him an help meet for him" **(Genesis 2:18).**

God's original and unchangeable intention is to use the institution of marriage as a platform to give you an opportunity to have a

> Marriage is not an end in itself but a means to an end.

"suitable" helpmate, encouragement, and companionship by your side as you journey through life fulfilling your God-given purpose and destiny. It is your purpose that demanded and warranted your marriage. Your marriage is a tool of your purpose.

When a person does not have this true, foundational perspective about marriage, he or she can become vulnerable to errors. With a distorted view of God's principles, these individuals are inevitably tossed back and forth by several winds of "convenient" ideas about marriage. It becomes very easy to get it all wrong, put the cart before the horse and to major in the minors or minor in the majors.

In this present and complex world of information overload, every young person is faced with a plethora of distractions, subtle deceptions, and ungodly permissions. Surprisingly, many of the individuals and institutions entrusted with the responsibility to uphold godly spiritual and moral standards are now the very culprits of decaying moral standards. This is actually a worrisome development and disturbing evidence that the Christian family and the church leadership are becoming compromised.

The clock shows time and the compass shows direction. My heartfelt prayer is that God will use this material to guide you to make right, timely, and godly choices in your marital relationship and beyond to secure a glorious destiny both in this life and in the life to come. Amen.

INTRODUCTION

Chapter 1
DATING

Dating without the intent of getting married is like going to the grocery store with no money. You either leave unsatisfied or you take something that isn't yours. **- Jefferson Bethke**

To have a date is to schedule a time to meet with and get together one on one with your friends, especially those of the opposite sex. Dating can be defined as the process of getting to meet and relate with people of the opposite sex for the purpose of friendship and without any commitment or strings attached. Practice makes perfect. Consequently, in the environment of dating, young people get to learn about the opposite sex—how they feel, think, behave and react to issues.

To a carpenter, everything is a nail. Likewise, a lady might think that everybody in the world thinks intuitively or emotionally until she starts socializing with men, especially in a dating environment. She then realizes that men don't see, think, or feel like women do, not because women are right and men are wrong or vice versa, but simply because they are different.

> Two people's opinions, perspectives, and actions can be right, yet, different.

The dating period is a time some young people will discover, probably for the first time, that in the world of human relationships certain answers to questions cannot be simply categorized as "right" or "wrong," black or white. In the real world with real people and real life issues, we do have cases that are neither black nor white but shades of gray. Two people's opinions, perspectives, and actions can be right, yet, different. For example:

DATING

1. Is right or wrong to eat your meat first or last when having dinner?
2. When you use toothpaste, is it right or wrong to press the tube at the bottom or in the middle?
3. When you hang your clothes in the wall robe, should the hanger be facing the inside or the outside?
4. A young intending couple was trying to decide and agree on the number of kids they should have when they got wedded. Is it right or wrong to have two or to have four?

Although these questions seem to be trivial, the issues involved have rocked some marriages at their very foundation. All of these matters call for a change in thinking, maturity, flexibility, tolerance, acceptance, and the ability to respectfully relate to people even when they have different opinions, perspectives, and feelings about an issue.

You may have a passionate love for slow songs and

someone else may be passionate about fast songs. Less experienced and immature people can insist that because they love slow songs, they are the best and the only songs to be listened to. This is why domineering and stubborn people who hardly shift ground and who always want to have it their own way are difficult to live with and create unhappiness in marriage.

12 GUIDELINES FOR SAFE DATING

Dating requires a high level of discipline and fear for God. It also demands that for your safety and to maintain purity in the relationship, you operate within the God-given standards such as:

1. Not being alone together at home or in solitary places.
2. No kissing, petting, and sexual relationships.
3. No unnecessary giving and collection of gifts that can become a trap.
4. Avoid too frequent contact that can lead to infatuations and cloud your decision and judgment.

5. Be accountable to mature, godly mentors.

6. Only date godly, God-fearing people who share your beliefs and ideals—do not be unequally yoked.

7. Avoid going to places and events that are questionable and inappropriate for you as Christians.

8. Let no one play on your emotions.

9. Place everyone on an equal platform. Remember that this is still dating, not courtship.

10. Avoid situations or environments that can encourage sexual activities.

11. When you become distracted by your emotions and they start getting out of control, take a break.

12. Pray before making or accepting any date proposal.

BEFORE YOU ACCEPT A DATING PROPOSAL

Use the following as yardsticks for making or accepting a date proposal:

a. "*Do not be unequally yoked*" *(2 Corinthians 6:14).*

b. If the lifestyle of a person is not clear to you, check his or her friends.

c. The way you dress will determine the way you will be addressed.

"*By their fruits, you shall know them*" *(Matthew 7:16, 20).*

d. The Peace of God.

Clarify any fear or doubt you have about the person asking you out on a date.

"*The peace of God that passes all understanding...*" *(Philippians4:7).* |

10 QUESTIONS TO ASK ON YOUR FIRST DATE WITH A GUY OR A GIRL

1. ABOUT GOD

What do you love most about God?

This question will help you to know and understand where they are in there spiritual journey and their relationship with God.

2. MATE MATERIAL
What are you looking for in a mate?
This will help you to understand your dates expectation, what spouse's role will be and what family life will look like.

3. ABOUT CAREER
What are your career plans?
This question will help you to know about their educational pursuit, career pursuit and plan for the future.

4. ABOUT HOBBIES
What do you do during your free time... like a hobby?
This question will help you to know what occupies there time.

5. ABOUT CHURCH & MINISTRY

What ministries are you involved with in your church?

This question will help you to know if they are active member of a local church. It will also help you to know there state of mind about giving back through volunteer services.

6. ABOUT FAMILY

How is your relationship with your family?

There relationships and interaction may give you an idea of how they treat others. It might also help you to spot the red flag of a challenging or complex family background.

7. ABOUT KIDS

Do you have kids?

This question will help you know about their past relationships, prepare you to be in a child's life and help you determine if they are in the habit of making babies but not commitment

8. ABOUT FRIENDS

Who is your best friend? Which group of friends do you like to hang out with?

This will help you know the kind of friend they keep or hang out with. It might also give you deeper insight about who your date is. "Show me your friends and I will tell you who you are."

9. ABOUT MUSIC

What type of music do you enjoy listening to?

The theme of the music will give you a glimpse into their mindset and the culture that is influencing there lifestyle.

10. ABOUT ROLE MODEL

Who are you role models and why?

This will give you an idea of where they want to be and who they want to be like.

11. ABOUT BOOKS

What type of book do you enjoy reading? Who is you best author?

It will give you an ideas of the though leaders that are shaping their thoughts, belief and mindset.

12. ABOUT SELF DISCLOSURE

Is there anything you think I should know about you?

This will give them the opportunity to tell you something about themselves that you should know ahead of time. It will also help you to determine how authentic they are.

4 KINDS OF BOUNDARIES THAT CAN KEEP YOU SAFE IN DATING RELATIONSHIPS

Boundaries are like our personal property lines in relationships. They are meant to protect you and keep you safe from invasiveness.

It is important that you set your dating boundaries before you need them. There is no lifetime

DATING

commitment during the dating phase of a relationship, so it's important not to bond physically,

> It is important that you set your dating boundaries before you need them.

spiritually, emotionally and sexually in the same way you would if you were married. Boundaries don't will keep

Do not shift the ancient landmark

1. Personal boundaries

- It will promote purity
- It promotes individual independence.
- It will help you protect your space and privacy from invasiveness.
- It will protect from unnecessary pressure or coercion in a dating relationship
- It will protect from a kind of control that in inappropriate in the context of a dating relationship
- It will promote relational safety.
- It will give you the courage to say "no" whenever it is necessary.

2. Emotional boundaries

- It will help you not to reveal too much too early
- It will help you maintain your time with other friends
- It will help you to maintain your spiritual relationship with God
- It helps you establish commitment before you start talking about the future together.
- It will help you to demonstrate emotional wisdom with feelings towards you date.
- It will help you not give any one your whole heart too early in a dating relationship.
- It will help you to say "no" when you are being asked to do things that don't feel right.

3. Spiritual boundaries

- It will protect you from feeling guilt and conviction about displeasing the Lord in my then-current relationship.
- It will help you to retain space for yourself spiritually so that you can maintain you individual

relationships with God and the church that do not depend on your dating relationship

- It will protect you from creating a deep spiritual bond with another person that can make it much harder to part ways even when parting ways is in both parties' best interest.

- It protects you from the level of intimacy that comes with spiritual bonding that a dating relationship is not equipped to handle.
- The emotional intimacy that comes from intense spiritual connection is not intended for dating relationship
- You don't have to move churches. You don't have to switch small groups.

It will help you to keep your spiritual sensitivity so that you can make decisions motivated by the desire to honour God first, not yourself or you dating partner.

4. Sexual boundaries

- It will protect you from engaging in physical intimacy outside of marriage

Practical boundaries to consider:

Physical contact - What kind of touching is OK and what is not?

Alone time - Is it OK to be alone in a room together or does that create too much temptation?

Curfew - Is there a certain time in the evening that you need to stop being together or talking on the phone?

Social activities - Are there certain parties, social activities or group gatherings that you need to avoid to limit temptation?

Media - Are there certain television shows, movies, music or printed material that take your mind to the wrong place?

DATING

I believe the Bible to teach that all sexual activity outside of marriage is sin, and all romantically oriented physical activity is sexual activity. In my view, this includes premarital kissing. **- Scott Croft**

Lessons Learn & Action Points

Chapter 2
ENGAGEMENT

As a general definition within the context of dating, engagement can be said to be a *joint* or *mutual* decision by a man and a lady to be *exclusively* committed to each other in a relationship with an ultimate purpose and intention to be married as husband and wife. It usually comes about as a result of dating. However, there are exceptions - in many instances, people have only met a few times at distance before they were engaged to each other.

Notice the word "joint" and "mutual" decision. These are very important to the definition of engagement. These words suggest a partnership, an agreement between the man and woman. In other words—it takes two to tango. Also, notice that the ultimate purpose and objective of being engaged is marriage, not for fun and self-defilement.

Sometimes, despite the most genuine intentions, not all engagements will end in marriage. This may create pain and heartbreak for the couple, but it is often said that a broken relationship, engagement or courtship is better than a broken marriage.

> Sometimes, despite the most genuine intentions and effort, not all engagements will end in marriage.

Engagement is different from dating in that it takes the focus away from relating generally to several members of the opposite sex as your friends to relating specifically and exclusively to one person as your intending spouse.

Engagement requires more discipline and commitment to do the right things and avoid the wrong things because strong emotions are now involved. More than ever before, you need to enforce the golden rule of dating and courtship in the relationship. Also, notice the word "exclusive" in the definition, meaning in this context that when you are engaged to someone, you are no longer permitted to date any other person. You are not to share love and affection with someone else unless the engagement has been *officially* terminated.

Sharing love and affection with another "date" can be tagged as unfaithfulness, which is very wrong. It compromises the foundation of your relationship and prevents you from building a strong marriage. If you are presently being unfaithful to your intending spouse, desist immediately, repent and ask God for forgiveness. *"Righteousness exalts a nation, but sin condemns any people"* **(Proverbs 14:34).** Discuss the issue with a mature Christian friend,

> "Double dating" in courtship is the foundation for infidelity in marriage.

mentor or your pastor before your restitution with your fiancé or fiancée.

He who covers his sins will not prosper, but whoever confesses and forsakes them will have mercy.
(Proverbs 28:13, NKJV)

Remember, you are not permitted under God to *"double date."* If you are engaged to someone, you need to set definitive boundaries with every person of the opposite sex. It will also be helpful if you do not keep your engagement a secret. "Double dating" in courtship is the foundation for infidelity in marriage.

ENGAGEMENT

Lessons Learn & Action Points

Chapter 3
COURTSHIP

Courtship is the period of time between the engagement and the wedding. The day you and your intended spouse mutually agreed to be engaged to each other is the first day of your courtship. The last day of your courtship, as it were, is the day you stand before the marriage altar with your intended spouse and take your vows. *"Prove all things; hold fast that which is good"* (1 Thessalonians 5:21).

> There is more to an individual than the outward display.

Courtship is the period of time when an intending couple gets to "test drive" their relationship before the final commitment to marriage.

This is like test driving a car before making the final purchase commitment. Some cars can look good and bright on the outside but there are several things you will never discover about the car until you drive it. If you make your car purchases based only on what you see (external, physical or in a picture) then you should be ready for plenty of unpleasant surprises. It should be noted that "test driving" does not permit the level of intimacy that is exclusive to married couples.

There is more to an individual than the outward display.

The Lord does not look at the things people look at. People look at the outward appearance, but the Lord looks at the heart. - **(1Samuel 16:7).**

There are a lot of people whose level of charisma and talent can make you fall in "love at first sight." But sometimes, these same people lack the character to back up their charisma. So making a lifelong decision based only on emotions instigated by a charismatic display is too dangerous.

Courtship is the period of time when an intending couple gets to know each other and find out if they are compatible.
We noted previously that men and women are different. Even individuals of the same sex are also different. No two persons are alike. The courtship period is a time to discover your differences more closely and also to find out if you can effectively tolerate and manage those differences. Success in a marriage is not about marrying a perfect person but about marrying someone whose strengths complement your weaknesses and vice versa.

Compatibility is all about putting the round peg in the round hole. Having a successful marriage is about marrying a person whose weaknesses you can tolerate, endure, and manage. In actual fact, your spouse is your number one ministry project. Your responsibility is to encourage your partner to get better and better by developing his or her strength and overcoming his or her weaknesses. **Every one of us is a *work in progress* and the *room for improvement* is the largest room in the world.**

Some intending couples are so extremely different. They are so far apart on almost everything and every issue, just like the east is far from the west. Such people might not be able to reconcile their differences. *"Can two walk together except they agree?"* (Amos 3:3). When intending couples discover that they are too far apart to be reconciled on all or most issues, they might have to immediately see an experienced and godly marriage counselor or explore the rule of Ecclesiastes 10:10 : "*…but wisdom is profitable to direct.*"

Courtship is the time to discover each other's areas of strengths and weaknesses

Discovering your strengths and weaknesses is not for

the purpose of self-justification, giving of excuses, castigating or condemning each other. Rather, it is a time of discovering, recognising and reconciling your differences. This will go a long way to guide you in discovering God's purpose for bringing the two of you together to complement each other.

"For the invisible things of him from the creation of the world are clearly seen, being understood by the things that are made..." (Romans 1:20).

Courtship is a place of acceptance

It is accepting and tolerating your partner despite his or her weaknesses. You and your intending partner are human. Therefore, each of you must be humble enough to accept that you have strengths and weaknesses. You should also be willing and emotionally secure enough to accept constructive feedback from each other, rather than becoming resentful and defensive. You should become each other's mirror giving helpful feedback on your strengths and weaknesses. You should also be willing to make positive adjustments, rather than becoming incorrigible.

Courtship is a time to be supportive

It is a time of supporting and encouraging your partner and making proactive positive changes as it relates to your weaknesses. It is also a time to be supportive in whatever personal or family challenges your intending partner is going through.

Courtship is a time of discovery

It is the time you should be able to discover if your intending spouse is wearing a mask. You need to find out if you are dealing with a godly, truthful, genuine, sincere individual or an ungodly, pretentious liar and deceiver who want to take advantage of you.

"Beware of false prophets, which come to you in sheep's clothing, but inwardly they are ravening wolves" (Matthew 7:15).

"And no marvel; for Satan himself is transformed into an angel of light" (2 Corinthians 11:14).

The book *entitled, 21 Principles of Human Personality* by Femi Oyewopo is an invaluable resource that can help you discover yourself and your partner. In it, you will learn that there are three phases of the human personality.

We have also outlined them here to help you analyse the three phases of the personality of your intending spouse.

Phase 1: Inborn Personality:- The original personality of your intending partner when he or she was born.

Phase 2: Developed Personality:- The original personality of your intending partner when he or she was born as well as an amalgamation of his or her life experiences and what he or she has become from birth until now including: education, experience, knowledge, attitude, beliefs, values, and character. Your developed personality is the real you as you are presently. For your partner, it is also the real person as he or she is at this very moment.

Phase 3: Expressed Personality:- Who you portray yourself to be. It is who your intending partner portrays himself or herself to be.

> Deception is when your expressed personality is different from the real you

Deception is when your expressed personality is different from the real you - your developed personality. An example is the case of Jacob in the Bible who expressed himself to be Esau.

Jacob said to his father, "I am Esau your firstborn. I have done as you told me. Please sit up and eat some of my game, so that you may give me your blessing."
(Genesis 27:19, NIV).

Jacob's action is a perfect example of a person wearing a mask. It is the root of deception in marriage.

If you get married to a person based on an expressed personality, you may suddenly discover - you have gotten married to a stranger:

So Jacob stayed and worked for Laban for seven years. But it seemed like a very short time because he loved Rachel very much. After seven years Jacob said to Laban, "Give me Rachel so that I can marry her. My time of work for you is finished."

So Laban gave a party for all the people in that place. That night Laban brought his daughter Leah to Jacob. Jacob and Leah had sexual relations together. (Laban gave his maid Zilpah to his daughter to be her maid.)

In the morning Jacob saw that it was Leah he had slept with, and he said to Laban, "You have tricked me. I worked hard for you so that I could marry Rachel. Why did you trick me?"
(Genesis 29:20-25, ERV).

Learn from Jacob's lesson and take the time to:

1. **Seek God's guidance.**

God knows and sees what you cannot. When Samuel was going to anoint the wrong person as the second king of Israel, it was God who prevented him from making an error.

When Jesse and his sons arrived, Samuel saw Eliab and thought, "Surely this is the man who the Lord has chosen."

But the Lord said to Samuel, "Eliab is tall and handsome, but don't judge by things like that. God doesn't look at what people see. People judge by what is on the outside, but the Lord looks at the heart. Eliab is not the right man."
(1 Samuel 16:7, ERV).

God can reveal your real partner to you. The scripture says that in this world there are wolves in sheep clothing, and there are demons displaying themselves as angels of light.

2. Seek out the guidance and wisdom of godly mentors

Because of their experience with God, they may be able to clearly see deception and traps where you may be sensing an opportunity.

There is a way that seems right to a man, but its end is the way to death **(Proverbs 14:12).**

3. Resolve every conflicting information or character.

When you hear conflicting information about your intending partner, go to those who will not tell lies about the matter and get the real facts.

In the case of Isaac, Esau, and Jacob, Isaac was in doubt and asked Jacob if he was the right person. What he did was to ask the right question to the wrong person. He put himself in the position to be deceived. May you not do the same.

Isaac grew old, and his eyes became so weak that he could not see clearly. One day he called his older son Esau to him and said, "Son!"

Esau answered, "Here I am."

Isaac said, "I am old. Maybe I will die soon. So take your bow and arrows and go hunting. Kill an animal for me to eat. 4 Prepare the food that I love. Bring it to me, and I will eat it. Then I will bless you before I die." **(Genesis 27:1-4, ERV)**

So Jacob went to Isaac his father. Isaac felt him and said, "Your voice sounds like Jacob's voice, but your arms are hairy like the arms of Esau."

Isaac did not know it was Jacob, because his arms were hairy like Esau's. So Isaac blessed Jacob.

Isaac said, "Are you really my son Esau?" Jacob answered, "Yes, I am." **(Genesis 27:22-24, ERV)**

Get good advice before you start a war. To win, you must have many good advisors.

(Proverbs 24:6, ERV)

But test everything. Keep what is good,

(1 Thessalonians 5:21, ERV)

Lessons Learn & Action Points

Chapter 4
TRIANGLE OF SUCCESSFUL RELATIONSHIPS

*"I (Paul) have **planted**, Apollos **watered**; but God gave **the increase**" (1 Corinthians 3:6).*

A successful courtship can be defined as courtship that fulfills the real purpose for which God brought the two people (a man and a woman) together.

> To have a successful courtship, you need to bring God into the equation.

The fact that a courtship did not end in marriage does not make it a failure. The final yardstick for measuring success in life and in courtship is how well a person fulfills the will of God.

For example; as much as we desire and pray for long life, it is written that the days of our lives are numbered. So at the young age of 33 years old, Jesus Christ completed His assignment and went back to the Father. During the days of Jesus, some people termed His death a tragedy but to us, it was total submission to the perfect will of the Father to become the ultimate sacrifice for mankind.

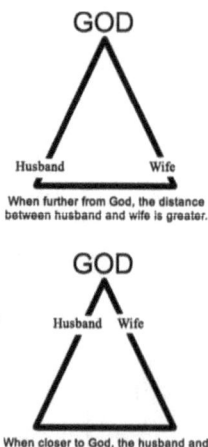

When further from God, the distance between husband and wife is greater.

When closer to God, the husband and wife will be closer to each other.

To have a successful courtship, you need to bring God into the equation. *"...for without me ye can do nothing"* (John 15:5).

TRIANGLE OF SUCCESSFUL RELATIONSHIPS

If you are presently courting, and God is not a part of your triangle, I counsel you to repent and invite Jesus to be the major part of your courtship triangle. You can find information on how to be saved in Chapter 16 of this book.

There are several reasons why you need God on your team:

1. Marriage is God's idea and no partner can make a marriage work by human ideas.

"And the LORD God said, It is not good that the man should be alone; I will make him an help meet for him" **(Genesis 2:18).**

2. You need God to persuade you that you are on the right track with the person you are engaged to so that the enemy will not make you doubt your choice in the days of storms and challenges.

The people who come to me, who listen to my

teachings and obey them—I will show you what they are like:

They are like a man building a house. He digs deep and builds his house on rock. The floods come, and the water crashes against the house. But the flood cannot move the house, because it was built well.

"But the people who hear my words and do not obey are like a man who builds a house without preparing a foundation. When the floods come, the house falls down easily and is completely destroyed."
(Luke 6:47-49, ERV)

2. You need the spirit of God to reveal whatever is hidden from you about your intending partner. He will keep you from error or deceit. He will guide you into all truth.

There is a way that people think is right, but it leads only to death. ***(Proverbs 14:12, ERV)***

TRIANGLE OF SUCCESSFUL RELATIONSHIPS

Trust in the Lord with all your heart and lean not on your own understanding; in all your ways submit to him, and he will make your paths straight.
(Proverbs 3:5-6, NIV)

4. Your best efforts amount to nothing without the help of God.

Unless the Lord builds the house, the builders labor in vain. Unless the Lord watches over the city, the guards stand watch in vain. **(Psalm 127:1, NIV)**

5. Unless your relationship is built on the solid rock, it cannot withstand the test of time.

Nevertheless, God's solid foundation stands firm.....
(2 Timothy 2:19, NIV)

6. It is only God who can keep you from falling. You need His help not to fall into trouble and sin during your courtship.

"Now unto him that is able to keep you from falling,

and to present you faultless before the presence of his glory with exceeding joy…" ***(Jude1:24).***

"And now, brethren, I commend you to God, and to the word of his grace, which is able to build you up, and to give you an inheritance among all them which are sanctified" ***(Act 20:32).***

TRIANGLE OF SUCCESSFUL RELATIONSHIPS

Lessons Learn & Action Points

PART B

Types of Courtship

Chapter 5

COURTSHIP 1: WRONG COURTSHIP

Wrong courtship is the period of time spent in a relationship with the wrong person between your engagement and the date set for the wedding.

"Be ye not unequally yoked together with unbelievers: for what fellowship hath righteousness with unrighteousness? and what communion hath light with darkness?"
(2 Corinthians. 6:14).

> Do not allow emotions and human pressure to becloud you.

Examples of wrong courtship are:

10 TYPES OF COURTSHIP

1. A courtship with an unbeliever.
2. A courtship or relationship with a married man or woman.
3. A courtship with a divorced or separated person.
4. A courtship with a person who professes to be a believer but has a questionable character, lack of fear of God or ungodly habits like drinking, smoking, use of hard drugs, fornication, cultism, and others.

"….they which do such things shall not inherit the kingdom of God" (Galatians 5:21).

Some people do embrace the man-made rule that when two people are legally separated; they can get married to someone else. What the Word of God says is that people who are divorced are not permitted to remarry until either of the two dies

I tell you that anyone who divorces his wife, except for sexual immorality, and marries another woman commits adultery. **(Matthew 19:9, NIV)**

WRONG COURTSHIP

"It has been said, 'Anyone who divorces his wife must give her a certificate of divorce.'
But I tell you that anyone who divorces his wife, except for sexual immorality, makes her the victim of adultery, and anyone who marries a divorced woman commits adultery. **(Matthew 5:31-32, NIV)**

The Pharisees asked, "Then why did Moses give a command allowing a man to divorce his wife by writing a certificate of divorce[a]?"

Jesus answered, "Moses allowed you to divorce your wives because you refused to accept God's teaching. But divorce was not allowed in the beginning. I tell you that whoever divorces his wife, except for the problem of sexual sin, and marries another woman is guilty of adultery."

The followers said to Jesus, "If that is the only reason a man can divorce his wife, it is better not to marry."
(Matthew 19:7-10, ERV)

If you are in a courtship and you intend to be married to an unbeliever, no matter your reason and excuse, you are treading the wrong path.

There is a way that people think is right, but it leads only to death. **(Proverbs 14:12, ERV)**

This is what the Lord says: "Stand at the crossroads and look. Ask where the old road is. Ask where the good road is, and walk on that road. If you do, you will find rest for yourselves. But you people have said, 'We will not walk on the good road.'
(Jeremiah 6:16, ERV)

Everything can look cool, calm, and collected today, but He (God) that can disclose the end from the beginning says: "Do not be unequally yoked..."
(2 Corinthians 6:14) and that there is a way that seems right today but the end is destruction.

WRONG COURTSHIP

In the beginning, I told you what would happen in the end. A long time ago, I told you things that have not happened yet..... **(Isaiah 46:10, ERV)**

Do not allow emotions and human pressure to becloud you. Do not try to justify your actions against God's Word. It is written:

Of course not! Though everyone else in the world is a liar, God is not. Do you remember what the book of Psalms says about this? That God's words will always prove true and right, no matter who questions them. **(Romans 3:4, TLB)**

Do not say "I will convert him or her to become a believer." You are not the Holy Spirit who convicts and converts. And even when the Holy Spirit convicts, it is the free will of the person to accept or reject.

"Look! I have been standing at the door, and I am

constantly knocking. If anyone hears me calling him and opens the door, I will come in and fellowship with him and he with me. **(Revelation 3:20, TLB)**

Do not say to yourself, "Times have changed from the days of the Bible. So God Himself will understand."

Forever, O Lord, Your word is settled in heaven [stands firm as the heavens]. **(Psalm 119:89, AMPC)**

"Heaven and earth shall pass away: but my words shall not pass away" **(Luke 21:33)**.

"Jesus Christ the same yesterday, and today, and forever" **(Hebrews 13:8)**.

Do not say, "He or she is now born again and is following me to church." Be careful not to deceive yourself or to be deceived by an unbeliever pretending to be a believer so he or she can marry you.

WRONG COURTSHIP

Lessons Learn & Action Points

_____

_____

_____

_____

_____

_____

_____

_____

_____

_____

_____

_____

Chapter 6

COURTSHIP 2: PURPOSELESS COURTSHIP

A purposeless courtship is one that has no sense of direction because it never existed or was lost along the way.

"Where there is no vision, the people perish."
(Proverbs 29:18).

A courtship is purposeless when one or both parties have no true intention to get married. If you are in a courtship and your partner seems not to be truly interested in marriage, it is better you opt out because he or she is most likely wasting your time. Maybe your partner is interested in or is already seeing someone else.

A courtship is also purposeless if the people involved do not have well-defined goals and plans for their lives. A wise man said that if a lady introduces a young man as her future partner and the young man does not seem to have a future ambition, then what future is the lady partnering with?

> A courtship is purposeless when one or both parties have no true intention to get married.

A purposeless courtship can also be defined as a courtship where the two people involved do not know or have not discovered God's purpose for bringing them together in courtship. Where purpose is not known, abuse is inevitable.

Lessons Learn & Action Points

Chapter 7
COURTSHIP 3: CARRY OVER COURTSHIP

Carry over courtship is when a relationship between a man and a woman as unbelievers is *carried over* to become a "Christian courtship."

"Therefore if any man be in Christ, he is a new creature: old things are passed away; behold, all things are become new" ***(2Corinthians 5:17)***.

"What shall we say then? Shall we continue in sin, that grace may abound? God forbid"
(Romans 6:1-2a).

The foundations of sin cannot be used to build a successful godly marriage. That is the reason why God will not accept Ishmael as the son of promise, despite Abraham's request:

Then he (Abraham) asked God, "Why not let Ishmael inherit what you have promised me?"

But God answered: No! You and Sarah will have a son. His name will be Isaac, and I will make an everlasting promise to him and his descendants.
(Genesis 17:18-19, CEV)

You cannot build a godly relationship on an ungodly foundation.

Jesus told them this story: "No one takes cloth off a new coat to cover a hole in an old coat. That would ruin the new coat, and the cloth from the new coat would not be the same as the old cloth.

Also, no one ever pours new wine into old wineskins. The new wine would break them. The wine would

spill out, and the wineskins would be ruined. You always put new wine into new wineskins.
(Luke 5:36-38, ERV)

It is very dangerous to build a life time relationship on a weak and faulty foundation.

"If the foundations be destroyed, what can the righteous do?" **(Psalm 11:3).**

Any building that does not have a foundation cannot last the test of time.

That is why many people are enduring marriages today, not enjoying them. Many seem to be standing from an outward perspective, but are actually broken down inside.

Therefore everyone who hears these words of mine and puts them into practice is like a wise man who built his house on the rock.

The rain came down, the streams rose, and the winds blew and beat against that house; yet it did not fall, because it had its foundation on the rock.

But everyone who hears these words of mine and does not put them into practice is like a foolish man who built his house on sand. The rain came down, the streams rose, and the winds blew and beat against that house, and it fell with a great crash. **(Matthew 7:24-27).**

Lessons Learn & Action Points

Chapter 8
COURTSHIP 4: NICODEMUS COURTSHIP

The Holy Bible, in the book of John chapter 3, contains the story of a member of the Jewish ruling council named Nicodemus who came secretly by night to see Jesus.

A Nicodemus courtship is a relationship that is kept as a secret from those who have the right to know about it. When you are secretly involved in a relationship without the knowledge of your pastors, your spiritual fathers, and mothers, your biological parents or godly mentors around you, then you are involved in a Nicodemus courtship. Many times, when people want to perfect their act of deception, they tell the other party not to tell anyone about the relationship. It is only evil deeds that are kept in secret.

Everyone who does evil hates the light. They will not come to the light, because the light will show all the bad things they have done. **(John 3:20, ERV)**

This is the message we heard from Jesus and now declare to you: God is light, and there is no darkness in him at all. **(1 John 1:5, NLT)**

If that young man or lady is insisting that you keep your affairs secret just between the two of you, then you might be dealing with someone who is hiding something or has ungodly intentions.

> When you are on the verge of making very important decisions about your life, it is dangerous and foolish to do it all alone.

Also, when you are on the verge of making very important decisions about your life, it is dangerous and foolish to do it all alone. You should recognize and appreciate the fact that if you want to enjoy true peace in your relationship and marriage, you need the help of God.

"Trust in the LORD with all your heart, and lean not on your own understanding; in all your ways acknowledge Him, And He shall direct your paths" **(Proverbs 3:5-6).**

If you want to escape the trap of deception in your marriage and the error of marrying someone who is lying and pretending, you need the help of God.

There is a way that seems right to a man, but its end is the way of death. **(Proverbs 16:25).**

God will also use godly mentors around you to guide you from making errors, assist you in recognizing deception, and keep you from falling into the traps of the enemy.

Where no wise guidance is, the people fall, but in the multitude of counselors there is safety. **(Proverbs 11:14, AMPC)**

God will also use them to teach you wisdom as to how you can manage your relationship well, resolve conflict, keep away from fornication and make your courtship a success. Without godly counsel, we are all prone to fall into error and deception.

A wise man said that there are two extremes in life; one extreme is where you listen to *everybody* and the other extreme is where you listen to *nobody*. Either of the two extremes is not good for you.

> There are two extremes in life; one extreme is where you listen to *everybody* and the other extreme is where you listen to *nobody*.

Anyone who tells you that you should make your courtship a Nicodemus one has got some skeletons in his or her cupboard. If you are in such a relationship, you must discuss the situation with a mature, godly, and trusted mentor immediately. If not, you will be used and dumped by someone who is probably married but is pretending to be single, or someone who is dating other people apart from you.

No one, when he has lit a lamp, puts it in a secret place or under a basket, but on a lampstand, that those who come in may see the light ***(Luke 11:33).***

Lessons Learn & Action Points

_____
_____
_____
_____
_____
_____
_____
_____
_____
_____
_____
_____
_____
_____

Chapter 9
COURTSHIP 5: CLOSED COURTSHIP

This is a courtship where the two parties are not sincere or open to each other - the people involved are hiding a lot of important information. For example, if a sister is desperate or feels that she has "caught a big fish," she may go to any length to hide vital information in order not to "scare away" the "big catch." God is never a party to lies and deception.

"This is the message which we have heard from Him and declare to you, that God is light and in Him is no darkness at all" (1John 1:5).

10 TYPES OF COURTSHIP

No matter what your present situation is or what was in your past, the Bible says that God *maintains and secures your lot* and blessing in life.

O LORD, You are the portion of my inheritance and my cup; You maintain my lot. The lines have fallen to me in pleasant places; Yes, I have a good inheritance. **(Psalm 16:5-6)**.

Maybe, you are hiding or lying about your age. Maybe, you are telling him that the baby you had out of wedlock is your mother's last born. Maybe, you are hiding your HIV status. Maybe you are still writing your entry level exams, but you are telling her that you are the university. Maybe, you are married with children, but you are telling her that you are still single. Are you building your relationship with straws or with solid blocks? Are you building on the foundation of truth or foundation of lies and

> Are you building on the foundation of truth or foundation of lies and deception?

deception?

But everyone who hears these sayings of Mine, and does not do them, will be like a foolish man who built his house on the sand: and the rain descended, the floods came, and the winds blew and beat on that house; and it fell. And great was its fall.
(Matthew 7:26-27).

The courtship period is a time of getting to know yourself and your partner. It is a time to declare your "assets" and "liabilities." Truly, there are certain liabilities that require lots of consideration and the use of wisdom before they are declared. Such situations might require that you seek the counsel and guidance of a mentor whom the two of you trust and respect. Remember, righteousness exalts a nation.

"Righteousness exalts a nation, But sin is a reproach to any people" **(Proverbs 14:34).**

Are there any family challenges or generational issues in the family? Are there any financial or debt burdens? Are there any pending issues from past relationships? Are there any health challenges? The covenant of marriage is *"Till death do us part."* It should be based on facts and knowledge, not on deception.

"He who answers a matter before he hears the facts-it is folly and shame to him" **(Proverbs 18:13, AMP).**

Any liabilities revealed after marriage can cause irreparable damage to your marriage. There is nothing hidden that will not be revealed. It is a matter of "when" and not a matter of "if." The reality is, trust builds trust. Deceiving a person into making a lifetime covenant with you has negative consequences.

> There is nothing hidden that will not be revealed.

"Then Joshua called for them, and he spoke to them, saying, Why have you deceived us, saying, 'We are

very far from you," when you dwell near us? Now therefore, you are cursed, and none of you shall be freed from being slaves--woodcutters and water carriers for the house of my God" **(Joshua 9:22-23).**

Lessons Learn & Action Points

Chapter 10
COURTSHIP 6: CAPTIVE COURTSHIP

In this type of courtship, there is no mutual respect, rather, one person is in charge as the "master" and the other partner is like a "slave."

The binding emotion in this relationship is not love but fear.

"There is no fear in love; but perfect love casts out fear, because fear involves torment. But he who fears has not been made perfect in love" **(1Jonn 4:18).**

There are several causes of captive courtship:

1. A lady may be getting older and desperate.

2. One person in the relationship may be suffering from an inferiority complex or feels less qualified based on education, financial status, social status,

family background or for other reasons.

3. One person may have much less to offer in the relationship than the other. This can be referred to as a parasitic type of relationship where one person habitually relies on or exploits the other.

4. One person may have been a victim of several unsuccessful relationships and he or she is not willing to lose the present one.

In a captive courtship, the "servant" counts himself or herself privileged to be associated with the "master." It is important to understand that this is not a godly arrangement or concept and so it cannot lead to a happy and fulfilling marriage.

A wise man said that God did not form the woman from the head of the man so that she will not rule over him. God did not form the woman from the feet of the man so the man will not see her as a slave to trample upon her. Rather, God in His wisdom formed the woman from the ribs by the side of the man because God wanted her to be by his side as his *friend* and *companion*. God also formed her from the rib by his heart because God wanted her to be close and dear to his heart. God formed the woman by taking from the man so that the woman will not compete with him but complete and complement him.

A captive courtship does not reflect God's plan, purpose, and pattern in a marriage.

Husbands, love your wives, just as Christ also loved the church and gave Himself for her. **(Ephesians 5:25).**

No longer do I call you servants, for a servant does not know what his master is doing; but I have called you friends, for all things that I heard from My Father I have made known to you. **(John 15:15).**

In some instances, however, one person may remain

humble as a "servant" in a captive relationship until the wedding ceremony is concluded, after which, they will show their true "coolers." Most of the time such marriages do not work because they are not consummated in love but in fear, anger, bitterness, feelings of helplessness and plans for revenge.

It should also be noted that when you are in a relationship where you may be better off than the other person physically, spiritually, educationally, financially or social status, you should never use it against him or her, rather do what Jesus did for us by bringing us to his level in love and making us partakers of all the Father has given to him.

"In My Father's house are many mansions; if it were not so, I would have told you. I go to prepare a place for you. And if I go and prepare a place for you, I will come again and receive you to Myself; that where I am, there you may be also" **(John 14:2-3).**

Lessons Learn & Action Points

Chapter 11
COURTSHIP 7: UNCLEAN COURTSHIP

"Marriage is honorable among all, and the bed undefiled; but fornicators and adulterers God will judge" **(Hebrew 13:4).**

Unclean courtship is the type where all kinds of wrongdoings are being practiced. For example, kissing, petting, touching, and fornication. When people who are courting get involved in uncleanness, they separate God from their relationship. Just as sin separated Adam and Eve from God at the beginning, it continues to cause a separation between mankind and God today.

Behold, the LORD's hand is not shortened, that it cannot save; Nor His ear heavy, that it cannot hear. But your iniquities have separated you from your God; and your sins have hidden His face from you, So that He will not hear. **(Isaiah 59:1-2).**

It has also been discovered that a man's love, trust, and respect for a lady diminishes when he sleeps with her before they are legally married.

And he said to him, Why are you, the king's son, becoming thinner day after day? Will you not tell me? Amnon said to him, I love Tamar, my brother Absalom's sister. **(2 Samuel 13:4).**

Now when she had brought them to him to eat, he took hold of her and said to her, Come, lie with me, my sister.
But she answered him, No, my brother, do not force me, for no such thing should be done in Israel. Do not do this disgraceful thing!

UNCLEAN COURTSHIP

And I, where could I take my shame? And as for you, you would be like one of the fools in Israel. Now therefore, please speak to the king; for he will not withhold me from you.
However, he would not heed her voice; and being stronger than she, he forced her and lay with her. Then Amnon hated her exceedingly, so that the hatred with which he hated her was greater than the love with which he had loved her. And Amnon said to her, Arise, be gone! **(2Samuel 13:11-15).**

When a young man and lady in courtship start to sleep with each other, the likelihood that they will get married also reduces.

Lastly, fornicating weakens your ability to say "no" to infidelity and stay faithful to each other in marriage. If you do not want to marry a husband who will have sex with his secretary in the office, teach him to exercise self-control and wait until you are married to engage in sexual activities. If you do not want to marry a woman who will easily succumb to her bosses advances in the office, teach her to say "no" to sex when the two of you are yet to be married.

Much more than all of the above is the fact that your body is the temple of the Holy Spirit. Honour God and His commandments by not allowing your body and your marriage bed to be defiled.

Flee sexual immorality. Every sin that a man does is outside the body, but he who commits sexual immorality sins against his own body. Or do you not know that your body is the temple of the Holy Spirit who is in you, whom you have from God, and you are not your own? For you were bought at a price; therefore glorify God in your body and in your spirit, which are God's. ***(1 Corinthians 6:18-20).***

If you are presently involved in uncleanness either with your partner or someone else, God is using this medium to ask you to repent and forsake your ways:

UNCLEAN COURTSHIP

He who covers his sins will not prosper, but whoever confesses and forsakes them will have mercy. ***(Proverbs 28:13).***

He who is often rebuked, and hardens his neck, Will suddenly be destroyed, and that without remedy. ***(Proverbs 29:1).***

Today, if you will hear His voice, Do not harden your hearts. ***(Hebrew 4:7).***

Please say the following prayer:

My Father and God, I thank you because I know that you love me. ***I humbly*** *accept and confess my sexual sins to you. I am sincerely sorry for defiling my body, which is your temple. Please forgive me and give me the grace to stay faithful and clean until I am married to the partner you have chosen and prepared for me. In Jesus' Name. Amen*

If we confess our sins, He is faithful and just to forgive us our sins and to cleanse us from all unrighteousness. (1John 1:9).

UNCLEAN COURTSHIP

Lessons Learn & Action Points

Chapter 12
COURTSHIP 8: DRY COURTSHIP

I planted, Apollos watered, but God gave the increase. (1 Corinthians 3:6).

Dry courtship drains you and dries you up. It saps your energy, resources, peace, joy and your very life. This is a courtship that is not symbiotic, mutually beneficial or complementary - one party is a first class parasite. Any courtship that you are involved in that is draining you up physically, spiritually, mentally,

> Dry courtship drains you and dries you up. It saps your energy, resources, peace, joy and your very life.

emotionally or financially is a dry courtship that will lead you nowhere.

He who walks with wise men will be wise, but the companion of fools will be destroyed.
(Proverb 13:20).

There is a principle that is called "the elevator principle." It says there are two types of people in your life: those who lift you up and those who bring you down. Is your courtship lifting you up or bringing you down? Step out of elevators that are taking you to the basement of life and step into elevators that will take you to the heights of your dreams.

> There are two types of people in your life: those who lift you up and those who bring you down.

Remember, being a lifting elevator does not mean having all the money, the endless list of academic qualifications, the best job, or that your life will be perfect. Life's assets are both tangible and intangible. Therefore, you may not have a relationship that is filled with amazing material possessions, but one that is spiritually, emotionally and mentally wholesome.

> Parasites are lazy, visionless, aimless people .... who are going nowhere with their lives.

By faith we understand that the worlds were framed by the word of God, so that the things which are seen were not made of things which are visible.
(Hebrew 11:3).

*Who can find a **virtuous** wife? For her worth is far above **rubies**. (**Proverbs 31:10**).*

Do not let your adornment be merely outward-- arranging the hair, wearing gold, or putting on fine apparel--rather let it be the hidden person of the heart, with the incorruptible beauty of a gentle and quiet spirit, which is very precious in the sight of

God. (1Peter 3:3-4).

Being a lifting elevator is more about having the fear of God, the right attitude, the right dreams, the right plan to move from where you are to where you want to be and the hard commitment to success and excellence in life. With all of these and with God on your side, it is only a matter of time before you become the person of your dreams. With such inner qualities, where you are coming from or where you are now cannot stop you from where you are going. A wise man said: Success is 30% aptitude and 70% attitude. Your attitude will impact more on your altitude in life than your aptitude.

> Success is 30% aptitude and 70% attitude. Your attitude will impact more on your altitude in life than your aptitude.

Parasites are lazy, visionless, aimless people who are always procrastinating, full of excuses and who are going nowhere with their lives. All they want is to "get all they can, can all they get and spoil the rest" **(Rick Warren).**

The lazy man will not plow because of winter; He will beg during harvest and have nothing.
(Proverb 20:4).

Beware of such people when you are making a decision on whom to spend the rest of your life with.
"Two are better than one... " (Ecclesiastes 4:9). This means that your relationship should make your life better and not bitter.

Lesson Learn & Action Points

Chapter 13
COURTSHIP 9: ARRANGED COURTSHIP

"Now Jacob loved Rachel; so he said, I will serve you seven years for Rachel your younger daughter. So Jacob served seven years for Rachel, and they seemed only a few days to him because of the love he had for her. **(Genesis 29:18, 20).**

Now it came to pass in the evening, that he took Leah his daughter and brought her to Jacob; and he went in to her. And Laban gave his maid Zilpah to his daughter Leah as a maid. So it came to pass in the morning, that behold, it was Leah. And he said to Laban, What is this you have done to me? Was it not for Rachel that I served you?

10 TYPES OF COURTSHIP

Why then have you deceived me? And Laban said, It must not be done so in our country, to give the younger before the firstborn. **(Genesis 29:23-26)**.

Arranged courtships are usually organized by the families or friends of the persons involved. These individuals may know within themselves that it is not the right choice and definitely not what they want. But for a variety of reasons may decide to remain in the relationship or just play along. Perhaps, they are afraid to disappoint those who arranged the courtship, are getting older and desperate that this could be their last chance at getting married (particularly with ladies) or they may feel the person in the arrangement is a "big fish" or a "good catch."

If you are caught in such a situation, you should carefully contemplate the fact that none of those who did the arrangement will live with you in the marriage. You only have one life. Don't lock yourself into a relationship that will cause you a lifetime of pain, resentment, and regret. Understand, when you don't know what you want, everyone will force what they think is right for you down your throat. If you do not stand for something, you will fall for anything.

In Gen Chapter 29, Leah's marriage to Jacob was arranged. Throughout the lifespan of their marriage, Leah never really knew true love. Jacob was just managing and enduring her. Jacob even confronted Laban, his father-in-law for forcing the wrong person on him. Jacob was ready to pay an extra price to get the woman he really loved.

"Then Jacob also went in to Rachel, and he also loved Rachel more than Leah. And he served with Laban still another seven years" (Genesis 29:30).

Jacob slept in Rachel's room so often that Leah had to exchange her son's mandrake for an opportunity to have Jacob in her room for just a night.

"And she said unto her, Is it a small matter that thou hast taken my husband? and wouldest thou take away

my son's mandrakes also? And Rachel said, Therefore he shall lie with thee to night for thy son's mandrakes" (Genesis 30:15).

God even affirmed that Jacob did not love Leah. Leah herself also knew that her husband did not love her.
*"When the LORD saw that Leah was unloved, He opened her womb; but Rachel was barren.
So Leah conceived and bore a son, and she called his name Reuben;[1] for she said, The LORD has surely looked on my affliction. Now therefore, my husband will love me" (Genesis 29:31-32).*

When there is no love in a relationship you cannot force it, it does not matter how well it was arranged, how much money was spent, how sexy or handsome you may be, or how much money you have—love cannot be coerced on a person.

The most serious dangers of arranged courtships and marriages are:

ARRANGED COURTSHIP

1. Your heart is not really involved or committed to the relationship.
2. You are just managing your partner.
3. Your partner might not be the type of person you really want.
4. It can lead to unfaithfulness and infidelity.
5. It can ultimately lead to a breakup of the marriage.

Every relationship has its own challenges but if yours is the result of an arranged courtship, chances are, it will not endure. Just like Adam blamed Eve for his disobedience when he said to God *"The wife you gave me..."* (Genesis 3:12), you will find yourself blaming others for every little challenge you go through in your relationship or marriage. If it was your choice, you may have been ready to take responsibility for your decision and its consequences.

"And the LORD God caused a deep sleep to fall on Adam, and he slept; and He took one of his ribs, and closed up the flesh in its place.

Then the rib which the LORD God had taken from man He made into a woman, and **He brought her to the man**" *(Genesis 2:21-22).*

"He who **finds a wife** *finds a good thing, And obtains favor from the LORD.* **(Proverb 18:22)**.

ARRANGED COURTSHIP

Lessons Learn & Action Points

Chapter 14
COURTSHIP 10: BALANCED COURTSHIP

Having a balanced courtship is like a living on a balanced diet—your growth is normal, you are healthy and you live long. A balance courtship has the following characteristics:

1. **Pure**—not unclean where the bed is defiled.

2. **Open**—not a closed courtship where vital information is hidden or covered with lies.

3. **Purposeful**—not an aimless and visionless courtship that leads nowhere.

4. **It is the right relationship** because it is not unequally yoked with an unbeliever or a married man or woman.

5. **It is built on a good foundation**, not one that is

poorly structured, faulty or weak as that of a carry-over courtship.

6. Free not a master-slave relationship.

7. Beneficial— not a parasitic and diminishing relationship.

8. It is your right choice of the right and godly partner that God has ordained for you.

Lessons Learn & Action Points

_____
_____
_____
_____
_____
_____
_____
_____
_____
_____
_____
_____
_____
_____

Chapter 15
HOW TO HAVE A BALANCED COURTSHIP

1. Be prayerfull

2. Trust God. Wait for Him. Do not give into fear and anxiety. Do not run ahead of God. Trust His good plans and timing for you.

3. Commit totally and absolutely to God's plan, will, and purpose for your life.

4. Do not compare yourself to others. You are unique, equally so are the times and seasons of your life. We are not mass produced human beings. We are all custom-built by God. People who compare themselves with themselves are not wise.

5. Be humble and courteous. Courtesy will open any door. Backup your charisma with character. Charisma will open doors for you, but it is only character that

can keep that door open.

6. Maintain the right attitude. Your attitude will determine your altitude in life. You cannot rise higher than your highest thought. You cannot grow bigger than your biggest thoughts. You cannot sink deeper than your lowest thoughts

7. Keep the right company. You will ultimately become like the company you keep. If you cannot change your friends, then change your friends. He who walks with the wise shall be wise. If an eaglet grows among chickens, she will end up crawling rather than flying.

8. Shun ungodly advice. Do not follow the advice of ungodly people. Seek out godly mentors, read good and inspiring books and learn to listen to the Holy Spirit for guidance and direction.

9. Be hardworking. The only alternative to hard work is a hard life. The choice is yours to make. You can pay now and play later or you can play now and pay later. Again, the choice is yours. But Solomon advised, "It is good for a young man to bear his

burden in the days of his youth" *(Lamentations 3:27)*.

10. Be ambitious and visionary. Aim high. Think Big. Set Goals. Go for Excellence. Detest mediocrity. Decide not to settle for less than your best. Become all that you can be. Express your full potential.
Remember that the room for improvement is the largest room in the world.

11. Develop yourself. If you want to marry a queen, strive to become a king.

Lessons Learn & Action Points

Chapter 16

HOW TO BE SAVED

If you haven't known God personally, here are four principles that will help guide you into a relationship with him:

1. GOD LOVES YOU AND CREATED YOU TO KNOW HIM PERSONALLY.

The most well-known verse in the Bible says, *"God so loved the world, that he gave his only Son, that whoever believes in him should not perish but have eternal life"* - **(John 3:16, ESV).**

You see, this life is not the end of us. This life is preparation for eternity. We have the freedom to decide where we want to spend eternity: with God or apart from God.

God thinks you're so valuable that he wants to spend eternity with you! The Bible says, *"Now this is eternal life: that they may know you, the only true God, and Jesus Christ, whom you have sent"* - **(John 17:3)**.

He planned the universe and orchestrated history, including the details of our lives, so that we could become his friends.

So, what prevents us from knowing God personally?

2. MAN IS SINFUL AND SEPARATED FROM GOD, SO WE CANNOT KNOW HIM PERSONALLY OR EXPERIENCE HIS LOVE BECAUSE OF OUR SIN.

The Bible says, *"All have sinned and fall short of the glory of God"* - **(Romans 3:23)**.

Visualize God in heaven and man on earth, with a great gulf separating the two. Man is continually trying to reach God and establish a personal relationship with him through his own efforts, such as a good life, philosophy, or religion—but he inevitably fails.

The Bible says, "*The wages of sin is death* [separation from God]" **(Romans 6:23)**. The third principle explains the only way to bridge this separation.

3. JESUS CHRIST IS GOD'S ONLY PROVISION FOR MAN'S SIN. THROUGH HIM ALONE CAN WE KNOW GOD PERSONALLY AND EXPERIENCE GOD'S LOVE.

JESUS DIED IN OUR PLACE.

"God demonstrates his own love for us in this: While we were still sinners, Christ died for us"
- **(Romans 5:8 NIV)**.

HE ROSE FROM THE DEAD.

"Christ died for our sins, just as the Scriptures said. He was buried, and he was raised from the dead on the third day, just as the Scriptures said. He was seen by Peter and then by the Twelve. After that, he was seen by more than 500 of his followers at one time..."- **(1 Corinthians 15:3-6, NLT).**

HE IS THE ONLY WAY TO GOD.

"Jesus said to him, 'I am the way, and the truth, and the life; no one comes to the Father, but through Me'"- **(John 14:6 NASB).**

Visualize now that God has bridged the gulf that separates us from him by sending his Son, Jesus Christ, to die on the cross in our place to pay the penalty for our sins. Yet it's not enough just to know these truths...

4. WE MUST INDIVIDUALLY RECEIVE JESUS CHRIST AS SAVIOR AND LORD; THEN WE CAN KNOW GOD PERSONALLY AND EXPERIENCE HIS LOVE.

WE MUST RECEIVE CHRIST.

"As many as received him, to them he gave the right to become children of God, even to those who believe in his name" - **(John 1:12 NASB)**.

WE RECEIVE CHRIST THROUGH FAITH.

"It is by grace you have been saved, through faith- and this not from yourselves, it is the gift of God- not by works, so that no one can boast" - **(Ephesians 2:8–9 NIV)**.

WHEN WE RECEIVE CHRIST, WE EXPERIENCE A NEW BIRTH.

The Bible tells of how a man named Nicodemus experienced a new birth through Christ:

There was a man named Nicodemus, a Jewish religious leader who was a Pharisee. After dark one evening, he came to speak with Jesus. "Rabbi," he said, "we all know that God has sent you to teach us. Your miraculous signs are evidence that God is with you."

Jesus replied, "I tell you the truth, unless you are born again, you cannot see the Kingdom of God." "What do you mean?" exclaimed Nicodemus. "How can an old man go back into his mother's womb and be born again?"

Jesus replied, "I assure you, no one can enter the Kingdom of God without being born of water and the Spirit. Humans can reproduce only human life, but the Holy Spirit gives birth to spiritual life. So don't be surprised when I say, You must be born again. The wind blows wherever it wants. Just as you can hear the wind but can't

tell where it comes from or where it is going, so you can't explain how people are born of the Spirit."
- (John 3:1-8, NLT)

WE RECEIVE CHRIST BY PERSONAL INVITATION

Jesus Christ says, "Behold, I stand at the door and knock; if anyone hears my voice and opens the door, I will come in to him and dine with him, and he with me." - **(Revelation 3:20, NASB)**

Receiving Christ involves turning to God from self and trusting Christ to come into our lives to forgive us of our sins and to make us what he wants us to be. Just to agree intellectually that Jesus Christ is the Son of God and that he died on the cross for our sins is not enough. Nor is it enough to have an emotional experience. We receive Jesus Christ by faith, as an act of our free will.

HOW YOU CAN RECEIVE CHRIST RIGHT NOW BY FAITH THROUGH PRAYER

Prayer is just talking with God. He knows your heart, so don't worry about getting your words just right. Here is a suggested prayer to guide you:

Lord Jesus, I want to know you personally. Thank you for dying on the cross for my sins.

I open the door of my life and receive you as my Saviour and Lord.
Thank you for forgiving me of my sins and giving me eternal life.
Take control of my life. Make me the kind of person You want me to be.

Does this prayer express the desire of your heart? If it does, pray this prayer right now, and Christ will come into your life as promised.

Did you pray to receive Christ just now?

If so, Congratulations! Luke 15:7 says that when one sinner accepts Jesus Christ as his or her Saviour the angels rejoice. So there's a party going on in heaven right now over your decision! Remember this date as your "second birthday," the day you were born into a new life in Christ! You have God's Word that he answered your prayer.

The Bible promises eternal life to all who receive Christ: *"God has given us eternal life, and this life is in his Son. He who has the Son has the life; he who does not have the Son of God does not have the life. I write these things to you who believe in the name of the Son of God so that you may know that you have eternal life"* - **(1 John 5:11–13 NIV).**

Thank God often that Christ is in your life and that he will never leave you. - **(Hebrews 13:5).**

You can know on the basis of his promise that Christ lives in you and that you have eternal life from the very moment you invited Him in.

DOWNLOAD THE TOOLBOX FREE

Just to say thanks for buying my book,
I would like to give you the
Ultimate Self Discovery Toolbox 100% FREE!

TO DOWNLOAD GO TO:

http://femioyewopo.com/21ipop_toolbox

Thank you

Thank You For Reading My Book!

I really appreciate all of your feedback, and
I love hearing what you have to say.

I need your input to make the next version of this book and my future books better.

Please leave me a helpful review on Amazon letting me know what you thought of the book.

Thanks so much!!
~ Femi Oyewopo

Practical Life Story

Do you have a real life story that is a proof of one or more types of courtship in this book?

Will you like so share your story with me?

Kindly send your story to:
femi@femioyewopo.com

"We are all pencils in the hand of God."
~Mother Teresa

END NOTE

www.ingramcontent.com/pod-product-compliance
Lightning Source LLC
Chambersburg PA
CBHW032041290426
44110CB00012B/900